LEAN STONE PUBLISHING

"Turn the Page And Live a Better Life"

www.leanstonebookclub.com

By reading this document, the reader agrees that under no circumstances are we responsible for any losses, direct or indirect, which are incurred as a result of the use of information contained within this document, including, but not limited to, —errors, omissions, or inaccuracies.

Canada

Canadian History: From Aboriginals to Modern Society: The People, Places, and Events That Shaped the History of Canada and North America

Table of Contents

Introduction

Canada is the homeland of equality, justice, and tolerance. (Kim Campbell)

Canada's history begins with the coming of the first Paleo-

Indians. Before the coming of the first European on Canadian ground, the land has been inhabited by a wide range of groups of Aboriginal peoples.

They established particular trade networks, spiritual beliefs and social hierarchies that defined their culture. Although the presence of these peoples has been discovered merely through historical investigations, the tribes that remained had influenced this country's history and development.

The late 15th century, when both French and British explorers discovered the Atlantic coast would bring massive changes in Canada. The colonization period followed, which significantly left its mark on the country's evolution and culture.

After the Seven Years' War in 1763, France had to give most of its colonies in North America to Great Britain. Afterward, Canada was established as a federal dominion comprising of four provinces. It was only in 1931 that Canada managed to achieve its status of independence, with the Statue of Westminster. Nevertheless, this act was finished in the Canada Act of 1982.

Over the years, the Canadian history has come to incorporate specific elements of Aboriginal, British, French and other immigrant traditions. That is one of the aspects that make the Canadian culture unique and beautifully diverse. After the two World Wars, Canada was the first country that would incorporate multiculturalism as an official policy.

Canada is renowned today for its natural social diversity and its devotion to respecting the principles and importance of multiculturalism, which is a quintessential element in a modern society.

Canada's history is rich and intriguing. It is a story that includes accommodation, union, division, and conflict. Not only that Canada is conveyed as being a multicultural society, but it is also a multinational one. And that has been largely determined by its course of history.

Embark with me on the road to finding out what made Canada what is today: the primary elements that structured its culture and society. This book accounts for an introduction to Canada's far-reaching history, intending to expand your knowledge.

Chapter 1 - The First Inhabitants of North America

At the moment, Canada is recognized as an important multicultural country, being the home to numerous immigrants belonging to different ethnic and religious groups. Nevertheless, a couple of centuries ago, the only people inhabiting this land would be the Aboriginal people of Canada. What does *aboriginal* mean? Aboriginal stands for *original inhabitants,* the people who first dwelled on this territory.

That being said, who were the first inhabitants of North America – Canada, to be more precise? Where did they come from and how did they develop, over time?

The First Signs of Human Settlements

According to studies, the human colonization of North America by the Clovis culture goes back to more than 13,000 years ago. Archeological evidence highlights that people could have dwelt on the continent 14,700 years ago, presumably several millennia before that. The route taken by the first humans coming to North America is still debatable, but most of the evidence points to the Pacific coast.

In this situation, that would mean that the populations of people aimed at exploiting the marine sources by boat. Another theory might be that the first humans arrived in North America by walking across a land-bridge from Siberia to Alaska, approximately 15,000 years ago.

It is thought that they made their way through an ice-free corridor that was located east the Rocky Mountains. Still, this is one of the numerous theories.

The peoples that developed afterward left behind some of the most significant historical artifacts – spear points and stone tools that go as back as 13,000 years ago. That being said, the Clovis culture is considered to represent the ancestors of the native people living in North and South America.

The first people who used to live on North American territory were the pre-Dorset, Paleo-Indian, Clovis, and Plano cultures that foreshadowed the present-day Aboriginal peoples. The Old Crow Flats and the Bluefish Caves are renowned as the earliest sites of habitation. Archeologists have collected a range of elements such as pottery, bangles and projectile point tools that indicate distinct traditions, periods and lithic reduction styles.

During the Late Pleistocene, the Paleo-Indians also referred to as Paleoamericans, were the first that occupied the Americas. There is a range of items such as scrapers and projectile points that indicate early human activity.

The Clovis or Llano culture belongs to the larger Paleo-Indian culture, which emerged at the end of the last glacial period. *Plano cultures* include the hunter-gatherer communities of people that used to live in the Great Plains Area during the Paleo-Indian or Archaic period.

These people used to hunt bison antiques. They also utilized a range of projectile point tools. As for their diet, it encompassed raccoon, deer, coyote, pronghorn antelope, and elk. In order to preserve their food supply, the Plano people would keep the meat in animal fat and berries.

Records indicate that all the Paleo-Indian groups would live in a dynamic landscape, featured by Pleistocene flora and fauna. What is more, the regions were characterized by the presence of megafauna. Species such as mastodons, mammoths, giant ground sloths, giant bison, short-faced bears and sabre-toothed cats were commonly met at that time. In this direction, most of the establishments belonging to Paleo-

Indian groups include the remains of megafauna. It is needless to say that this has created the false impression that these peoples were dedicated to hunting exclusively large game.

For a given timeframe, this assumption was actually backed up by a diversity of preservation and identification issues such as the accelerated degeneration of small mammal, vegetal and fish remains in the archaeological records. Nevertheless, at the turn of the 21st century, after numerous excavations at important sites, some Paleo-Indians depended on a variety of plant and wild animal foods. That being said, a better characterization of the Paleo-Indians would be as generalized hunter-gatherers.

They also created containers from hides for the same reason. Since they had plenty of food sources, the human settlement developed quickly and spread towards the Western Hemisphere. The Paleo-Indians used to live in small groups; they weren't larger than fifty people. They were continually on the move, going after herds of big game.

According to official evidence, the Plano cultures occupied the Canadian territory between 9000 BC and 6000 BC. At first, they occupied the plains and later on reached the Northwest Territories, as well. As for the Pre-Dorset culture, it occupied the Eastern Arctic, being acknowledged as a Paleo-Eskimo culture. The Paleo-Eskimo, pre-Thule or Pre-Inuit culture emerged around 2500 BC and disappeared in 1500 CE.

Although scientists don't agree on where the First Nations people originate from, or how they got to North America, one thing is for sure: these peoples were genetically linked to people in parts of Asia. The main theory is that nomadic hunting peoples used to follow big animals for food and survival. As the ice sheets melted, these peoples spread out on the continent and evolved into different cultures to suit distinct environments.

Elements that Influenced the Development of Aboriginal Peoples

Typically, the features of Aboriginal cultures in Canada included civic and ceremonial architecture, trading networks, permanent settlements and complex societal hierarchies. Additionally, genetic studies point that the first people that inhabited Canada (the American Continent), developed from a singular ancestral population.

As the glaciers started to melt, people had the possibility of moving either south or east into Canada. In fact, the very first settlers are thought to have entered North America by hunting Pleistocene mammals such as musk ox, mastodons, wooly mammoths, steppe wisent, and giant beavers.

The unique diversity of vegetation, fauna, and climates has distinctively influenced the ancient cultures. Spiritual practices, language influences, and social life largely contributed to group identity. Anthropomorphism and animism have impacted indigenous religions. At the moment, ancient cultures are still identified by the distribution of archeological sites, manufactured items, and subsistence practices that highlight their cultural beliefs.

In 1000 BC, the climatic and environmental conditions were comparable to those encountered by European travelers. Although cultural patterns were still distinguishable, diffusion and innovation were the primary forces that encouraged the cultural change. For example, the introduction of pottery differentiates Old Copper peoples from previous cultures. Additionally, the woodland culture is recognized as a prehistoric culture featured by the construction of burial mounds, and the creation of various pottery styles. They would also raise beans, corns, and squash

Southern Ontario and the Northwest coast were densely

populated considering the presence of abundant resources and a type of land adequate for farming.

European explorers referred to the native people living in North America as the Indians (comprising of the Thule, the Dene, the Dorset and the Intuit). It is thought that about 500,000 to 2,000,000 people used to reside in this region.

To conclude, Canada's native peoples are separated into three broad categories: the Intuits, the Indians, and the Metis.

The Intuits originally lived in the Arctic. Their official language was Inuktitut, but it features distinct dialects that differ by region. They were the least populated group in Canada – about 45,000 Canadians identify themselves as being part of the Intuit tribe.

The first nations were referred to as *Indians* by Christopher Columbus when he first reached North America, as he assumed he entered India. The First Nations tribe spoke approximately 70 different languages.

And lastly, the Metis represent a group a people that resulted from the mixture of Native and European men and women. They have a unique culture that combines both European and Native elements.

Even though there aren't any comprehensive written records regarding the history of Canada's indigenous society before its contact with the Europeans, there is archeological proof. Apart from the archeological evidence, the oral traditions also construct a consistent image of the pre-contact period. That being said, there were 12 principal language groups among the people that are currently living in Canada, as follows: Iroquoian, Algonquian, Siouan, Kootenai an, Athabascan, Salishan, Tsimshian, Inuktitut, Wakashan, Beothukan, Tlingit, and Haidan.

Each of these groups features particular cultural and political divisions. For example, the Iroquoian people encompassed two primary subgroups, namely the Huron and the Iroquois. Furthermore, these groups were separated into smaller groups, and so on.

Additionally, before European contact, Canada represented noteworthy variations in means of subsistence, culture, tribal customs and laws, intertribal relationships, philosophies of trade, and so on. History teaches us that the Eastern Woodland Indians, such as the Petun, Iroquois, Huron established a unique subsistence economy of agriculture and hunting supplemented by trade. That being said, the construction of semi-permanent villages has been noted, fields were cultivated, trails were made accessible between villages, and the game was hunted. And that is not all. Among some of these people, there was a notable level of political organization.

Namely, both the Iroquois and the Huron shaped religious and political confederacies. What is more, they designed far-reaching trading systems as well as political collaborations with other groups. On the other hand, the peoples that were dwelling in the far north don't appear to have established significant political communities, according to archeological records. Meanwhile, the inhabitants of the Eastern Woodlands and the west coast designed complex social and cultural institutions.

One thing is worth noting though: the climate and the geography were primordial factors that influenced the development of the societies present in North America. However, the primary element the indigenous people had in common was that each group was politically independent and self-governing.

Common Misconceptions about the First Inhabitants of North America

1. They Were War-Hungry Savages

Media has created the stereotype of North America's indigenous people. The stereotype is portrayed in the following way: Tomahawk, feathers in the air, bow, and arrow, and an inborn eagerness to attack Europeans and newcomers. Nevertheless, that is far from being accurate, since numerous indigenous tribes in North America were genuinely peaceful.

What is more, some of the tribes have fought against the Europeans in order to protect their land. Although the Europeans were the ones that invaded their land, it was still the indigenous people that are conveyed as being eager to fight wars.

2. The Indigenous People Were Primitive, in Comparison with the Europeans

Probably the second most widespread misconception regarding the first inhabitants of North America is that they were primitive. Notwithstanding, the truth is that the indigenous people of North America were innovative in many respects, particularly in the realm of medicine. To be more precise, they have invented numerous natural treatments for distinct illnesses, many of which were actually adopted by Europeans.

That being said, when the first Europeans reached North America, they were astonished when they realized that the natives would recover from injuries and illnesses that they would consider fatal. In numerous ways, the remedies known by the natives were superior to the ones used and known by the immigrants.

They would use quinine from the bark of trees in order to treat malaria. Later on, scientists discovered that it could actually prevent malaria, as well. What is more, the indigenous people would use other tree barks to cure intestinal infections such as dysentery, which was quite commonly met at that time. Moreover, they provided the Europeans with a legit cure for healing scurvy. The medicine comprised of a combination of pine needles coming from an evergreen tree and other elements. The medicine included high levels of vitamin C, which was fundamental for that condition. Additional medicinal discoveries made by the indigenous people were: a cure for headaches, fever reducers, medicine for soothing muscles and pain killers for child birth.

Surprisingly, many of the ingredients incorporated into that medicine are still used till this day. For what it's worth, dental care is largely attributed to the native people of the American continents, as well. In North America, the natives would use sticks to wash their teeth.

The primary distinction between the healing methods used by the indigenous people and Europeans was that they considered spirituality to have played a fundamental role in the healing process. They believed that every element in nature was linked to spirituality.

They also assumed that one's spirituality could cause an illness or heal it. That's why, apart from treating the physical part of the suffering individual, they had to heal his/her emotional wellness as well, promoting harmony with the environment and the surrounding community. Apart from the herbal medicines, the community would reunite to help the ill by chanting, praying, dancing or organizing ceremonies.

Interesting Facts!

- The Iroquois used to celebrate a winter festival that resembled trick-or-treating. A group of teenagers would sing and dance around the village, being led by an old woman. They would stop outside people's houses and wait until they received presents.
- When an Iroquois woman was pregnant, she didn't eat turtles. This way, she would avoid her baby growing clumsy on land, similar to a turtle. Additionally, in Navajo communities, pregnant women used to untie their long braided hair and free animals such as horses. That was believed to create a free passage for when the baby would come.
- Indigenous people from the northwest, such as the Haida, used to construct totem poles that would reach 40 feet outside their homes to indicate their families' status. Typically, the pole would display birds or animals the family regarded as special. Additionally, totem poles served as memorials to the family's ancestors. Christians mistakenly believed that totem poles were actually statues of gods.
- There are 1,172,790 Metis, First Nations and Intuit people in Canada, who are referred to as Aboriginal. That accounts for 3.8 percent of Canada's total population.
- Ontario presents the largest number of aboriginal people at 242,495.
- During 1996 and 2006, the aboriginal population in Canada increased by 45 percent in comparison with the non-aboriginal population that grew by 8 percent.

If the Choice Were Yours

- Why do you think that the aboriginal peoples ended up inhabiting the current land occupied by Canada? What would you have done if the choice were yours? What are the main aspects that would have affected your decision?

Chapter 2 - Vikings in North America

Approximately 500 years before the coming of Christopher Columbus to the New World, a band of European sailors set foot on American ground. I'm referring to the Vikings – the greatest seafarers in history. They were fearless in sailing the cold waters of the North Atlantic, in dangerous and unexpected conditions. And of course, they reached North America, as well.

For starters, who were the Vikings? Where did they come from?

Also referred to as Norsemen or Northmen, the Vikings belonged to the Scandinavian seafaring warriors who colonized significant segments of Europe, from the 9th to the 11th century. Their influence has left a profound mark on European history. They were Swedish, Danish and Norwegian pagans that sought adventure overseas. They were in search of new lands to settle; lands which featured resources they could exploit.

The historical details about Norse Trips to Vinland (as the Vikings called North America) originate from two sources: *The Saga of Erik the Red* and *The Saga of the Greenlanders*. It is assumed that these epic Viking tales were recorded around 1200 and 1300 by scribes. Viking scholars have argued the accuracy of the Icelandic sagas – are they history, literature, or a combination of both?

According to archeologists, it's up to them to differentiate facts from fiction, as it cannot be presumed that the saga writers knew to tell the difference between the two. Names of places and people are confused, and the focus is placed depending on specific purposes.

Leif Eriksson the Lucky – The First Norse Explorer that Reached North America

There are distinct accounts that testify to Leif Eriksson's coming to Canada. Nevertheless, there are different elements that make it challenging for historians to separate between reality and fiction.

It is assumed that Leif was born around 960-970 A.D, being the second out of Erik the Red's three sons. Erik the Red was thought to have established the very first European Settlement in present-day Greenland. Erik the Red had actually been banished from Norway because of some crimes he had committed, according to the sagas. Hence, he settled in Iceland. Historians assume that Leif Eriksson was born and raised in Greenland.

Based on the sagas, the Norse began exploring the lands west of Greenland a few years after the establishment of Greenland's settlements. In 985, Bjarni Herjólfsson – a merchant, was blown off course and he noticed the presence of land, west of the fleet. Although he had seen the North American continent from a distance, he didn't set foot on the land.

Leif Eriksson was the one that conducted the first expedition to Vinland, fifteen years later. According to most accounts, Eriksson sailed from Greenland to Norway, somewhere around the year 1000. At that time, he served in the court of King Olaf I Tryggvason. He was, in truth, the one that converted Leif from Norse paganism to Christianity. As a consequence, Olaf appointed Leif to embark on a journey whose purpose was to convert other nations to Christianity. Even though Eriksson did eventually return to Greenland, the motives and details linked to his return route are debatable and remain uncertain.

His brother, Thorvald initiated another journey; nevertheless, he died as a result of a conflict with the Aboriginal inhabitants. Another brother – Thorstein wanted to follow, but unsuitable weather stopped him.

It was Thorfinn Karlsefni, Leif Eriksson's brother in law, who managed to deliver a successful trip to Vinland. It is assumed that the dates for these voyages were about the year 1000. The rest of the journeys took place during the following decade. Afterward, they stopped.

The Norse name for North America – Vinland – truly portrayed the reality. Archeological discoveries at L'Anse aux Meadows demonstrate that the Norse traveled south to areas in which grapes grew wild. In Norse society, wine was a truly cherished beverage, which was part of a lavish lifestyle. It also meant influence and power. Additionally, the area featured rich hardwood forests where timber could be harvested. They were conveyed as pure treasures by the Greenlanders who lacked forests.

The sagas feature the presence of Helluland, which means the land of flat stones, and Markland, which stands for the lands of forests.

By using the landmarks and routes described by Bjarni, Leif sailed approximately 1,800 miles to the west of the land. He wintered in 1001, in the proximity of Cape Bauld. In 1004, Thorvald Eriksson sailed to Vinland with a crew of 30 people, spending the winter at Lefi's camp.

It is believed that exploration was the primary purpose why the Vikings came to Vinland. For instance, the groups consisted primarily of men, as opposed to families. Additionally, the people who came on the journeys were chosen depending on their skills. There were also slaves, brought to do heavy work. The presence of few women is due to domestic purposes. There were approximately 20-30 people per ship, which contradicts settlement.

The settlement was given the name *Lefi's camp,* which, once again, indicates the nature of the stay. L'Anse aux Meadows has a lot in common with Lefi's Camp – being recognized as the basis for further exploration, as opposed to the homestead of emigrants.

In technical terms, L'Anse aux Meadows could be conveyed as a gateway to Vinland's resources. In the Norse society, the power of the chieftain was significantly influenced by the display of richness, goods and unexpected things brought from abroad expeditions. On that note, controlling trade and imports was quintessential for a chief.

Irrespective of the presence of distorted elements from the Greenlanders' Saga and Eric's Saga, for the most part, they complement each other with regards to the primary details linked to the expedition. The base camp was referred to as Straumfjord, which stands for Current Fjord, being situated in the northern part of Vinland, presumably in the proximity of Strait of Belle area. Another camp, which was used exclusively in the summer, was Hop, which stands for Lagoon. It is assumed that it was located in southern Vinland. In that area, excellent timber and grapes were harvested and shipped back to Greenland. What is more, the Norse had a range of conflicts with the aboriginal people there, as well.

Despite being the first European explorer to set foot on North American soil, Eriksson would never colonize the region, nor did his brothers, who reached Vinland after Eriksson. According to records, he actually returned to Greenland, where he tried to convert his parents to Christianity. His father wasn't receptive to the new faith. Nevertheless, he did succeed in converting his mother, who determined the construction of the first Christian church in Greenland, namely in Brattahild.

Was Vinland in Newfoundland?

It is hard to pinpoint Vinland's exact location because the details presented in the sagas are conflicting on some points. Although the sailing information indicates towards Newfoundland, the descriptions of abundant vegetation such as self-sown wheat, grain, as well as the discovery at L'Anse aux Meadows of butternuts points towards a more southerly position on the map.

The uncovering of the Norse habitation at L'Anse aux Meadows provided important support for those who assumed Vinland was located in Newfoundland. Notwithstanding, according to the findings, L'Anse aux Meadows seems to have been a small settlement encompassing no more than eight buildings. These could accommodate a maximum of 75 people. It is believed that the individuals who dwelled there were mostly sailors, blacksmiths, carpenters, hired hands or even slaves.

In fact, it is assumed that the settlement represented a base camp meant to repair and maintain Norse ships. Presumably, the settlement was also a base camp for organizing additional expeditions towards the south.

Artifacts belonging to Norse women had also been found there. Nevertheless, archaeologists agreed that the settlement had the purpose of a seasonal camp. Based on findings, it had never played the role of a permanent establishment, like the ones that had been found in Greenland.

As for Vinland's exact location, archeologists concluded that this wasn't a particular site, but rather a region that included Newfoundland, reaching the Gulf of St. Lawrence and coastal New Brunswick.

Why Didn't the Vikings Stay?

A common question regarding the coming of the Vikings to North America is why didn't they stay? That is an intriguing question, especially since the Vikings were skilled seamen and unrivaled raiders who populated Greenland and reached the British Isles and France, as well. What is more, evidence indicates that they were equipped with iron tools and weapons, which gave them a technological edge over North America's indigenous people.

It is needless to say that some explanations have been voiced in this regard. One of them is that there were too few of them to preserve the settlements. Additionally, the settlements were established for exploration reasons, functioning as gateways for bringing goods to their homeland.

What is more, Vinland was a remote location. The Norse voyages towards North America were uncertain and risky, as we can learn from the sagas. Plus, the Norse expeditions dealt with vigorous resistance from behalf of the native inhabitants. Although it is assumed that the Norse were more advanced than the natives, the small number of Norsemen in North America meant that this advantage was minimized.

In the early 11th century, the settlements in Greenland were in their early phase. In other words, they didn't have the wealth or the population to support any new colonies. Perhaps there could have been an incentive in this respect later on. But, at that time, the inhabitants were focusing primarily on their own survival, as opposed to concentrating on their expansion.

What is more, another reason why the Norse voyages to Vinland weren't long-lasting was that the new colony established in Greenland, which consisted of a few hundred inhabitants only, had no need of additional land. Plus, the abundant resources in Vinland were at a considerable distance. Vinland was as far from Greenland as was Norway. From what it's worth, most of the products they could get from Vinland were also available in Europe, where other essentials such as grain, iron, salt and spices were present.

Vinland was a feeble colony that wasn't capable of sustaining itself as economic, climatic and political conditions started to deteriorate.

Another popular theory is that climate change is the primary reason why the Vikings chose not to stay on American Territory. They imply that the western Atlantic could have become too cold – even for the Vikings.

As recently pointed, the sailing trips of Leif and Thorfinn took place in the first half of the 11th century when a climatic change has been recorded, known as the Medieval Warming. This timeframe was featured by scarce sea ice, long and warm summers. Notwithstanding, during the 12th century, the weather started to alter – the scholars refer to this period like the *Little Ice Age,* during which the *first frissons* were noted.

Additionally, during the 14th century, the colony experienced eight harsh winters in a row. 1355 was the year that recorded the worst and coldest winter of the century. If the Vikings had followed the strategy of the Inuit people, who would hunt ringed seal in the winter, perhaps they would have stayed in North America. Also, another hindrance could have been Greenland's small population.

Furthermore, the sea ice worsened the routes from Greenland to Iceland. In other words, the Little Ice Age presumably prevented Norse traffic to North America. Apparently, Iceland suffered a lot during this time, as well. By 1703, the food shortage and epidemics of smallpox and plague diminished Iceland's population to 53,000 – in 1205, there were approximately 150,000 inhabitants.

That being said, it's worth speculating how the history of the

West would have been if the weather wouldn't have changed so drastically, or if the Norse establishment in Greenland would have been larger. Perhaps the Norse populations in Greenland and Iceland would have expanded, and the Vikings could have stayed in North America. In plain English, if the temperatures would have been a bit more acceptable, part of North America would have spoken Norse.

To conclude, the Norse contact with Newfoundland was unforeseen, and their experience was short-lived. Even though the Vikings are considered to be the first Europeans that lived in North America, saying that they *discovered America* is an exaggeration. They reached a new land without actually discovering it. The European discovery of North America, in the sense of raising awareness of the existence of a *new world,* would have to wait until the coming of John Cabot.

Common Misconceptions about the Vikings

1. The Vikings Were Dirty, Wild People

Most movies portray the Vikings as being wild-looking, dirty, savage men that had no interest in their looks. Still, the reality is distinct. Truthfully, the Vikings were interested in their appearance. Archeologists have found a wide range of elements that indicate their focus on grooming. Viking Age excavations have indicated that the Vikings actually made soap. Plus, they would also use *ear spoons,* tweezers, and combs.

Apart from that, at that time, the Vikings had a reputation for excessive cleanliness, due to their custom of bathing once a week – on Saturdays. Even today, in the Scandinavian languages, Saturday is referred to as *washing day,* although the initial meaning is lost in modern speech. The bottom line is that the Vikings actually cared about their personal hygiene more than other peoples.

2. The Vikings Didn't Stay in North America because of the Aboriginal Peoples

It's true that the aboriginal peoples have fought against the Norse on several occasions. Nevertheless, that wasn't the only reason why the Vikings choose to leave Vinland. Probably, what determined them to leave was a combination of factors. Greenland was a young establishment, and it didn't have the means to sustain the colonization of a new land.

Additionally, the Vikings weren't interested in colonizing Vinland. The nature of their establishments was merely temporary, which indicates they only wanted to take riches back to their homeland. Plus, they constructed those settlements in Vinland in order to take the resources they didn't have back at home.

Interesting Facts!

- The Vikings were excellent boat builders, which is one of the primary reasons why they would explore new lands. The length of their boats ranged from 52 to 120 feet, and approximately 60 Vikings would fit into one boat. They were designed to be highly versatile so that they could be steered both through shallow rivers and high seas.
- The Norse took pride in physical power and strength. If a child was unable to fight and wasn't thought to be useful to the society, he/she was considered a burden. As a result, such children were often abandoned, thrown into the sea or left to die.

- Viking women had a range of fundamental rights, in comparison with other women from that era. That being said, they had the right to request a divorce, inherit property and reclaim their dowry in the case in which they ended a marriage.

If the Choice Were Yours

- What would you have done if you were in Leif Eriksson's shoes? Would you have chosen to colonize Vinland? Why?

Chapter 3 - The European Exploration in the 15-16th Century

In spite of the presence of Norse Settlements, when Europeans approached North America, in the late 15th century, they were uninformed regarding their predecessors' discoveries.

The European Exploration that is typical of the 15-16th century has taken place due to religious, scientific, military and commercial purposes. Additionally, the pursuit of trade, the satisfaction of curiosity, the spread of religion, and the wish for political power and security are other grounds for the European Exploration.

The contact between the aboriginal peoples of Canada and the Europeans has increased in the 15-16th centuries. Typically, the natives accepted the coming of foreign fishermen, as long as they concentrated on trade, and didn't try settling on their land.

Among the Europeans, the British and the French were the ones who had the most contact with the aboriginal peoples of Canada. Initially, the French were focused on the island of Newfoundland, Acadia, St. Lawrence Valley, Great Lakes, and Ohio Valley a bit later. In the meantime, the British occupied James and Hudson bays, and, later on, they would claim other parts of the land, as well.

John Cabot and Giovanni de Verrazano

It is speculated that the first ones that reached Newfoundland were some seamen from Bristol. This happened around 1480, foreshadowing Columbus's voyage that took place in 1492. Nevertheless, the first considerable evidence indicates to John Cabot's English expedition from 1497. At that time, explorers wanted to find a westward route to Asia.

Giovanni Caboto (John Cabot) was a renowned Genovese explorer appointed by England, under the reign of Henry VII. He gave Newfoundland the name of *New Island*. Additionally, he landed at Cape Breton, which is presently part of Nova Scotia, assuming that he discovered the northern coast of Asia – the Indes.

He claimed the territory in the name of the king. Although some historians consider John Cabot to be the first person who discovered today's Canada, he didn't institutionalize any colony. Nevertheless, Cabot did have a contribution in the equation. He informed the Europeans – English, Spaniards, Portuguese, and French of the presence of new territory.

In 1499, João Fernandes, who was Portuguese, explored Labrador and Newfoundland. It is considered that, two years later, his fellow countrymen have followed. According to historical maps, the territory was referred to as *Terra de Corte Real*. From that point onward, Portuguese fishers started to set up small bases on a coast they would name *Terra do Labrador*.

At that time, the name Lavrador or Labrador made reference to what they assumed to be a single expansion of land from Greenland to Newfoundland. As soon as they comprehended that Greenland was disconnected from the Canadian Coast by the Baffin Bay, the name Labrador would refer solely to the northeastern side of the continent.

Everything that remained after the Portuguese voyages is a range of establishments that carried Portuguese names such as Labrador, Bao Vista, Terra dos Buccalaos (Land of Cod), and others. Also, they started working with North Atlantic fishers. Nevertheless, they didn't colonize the area.

Giovanni de Verrazano was the one that started a scouting expedition to North America in 1524, on behalf of the King of France. As soon as he landed on the coast of North Carolina, he traveled to the Hudson River, then to Cape Breton Island. He gave the territory a new name: *Nova Gallia,* which translated means New France. Additionally, he named certain establishments: the Lorraine coast (New Jersey and Delaware Region), Angouleme (New York), the Vendome River (the Delaware), and others. Still, these names were temporary as Verrazano's voyages didn't result in colonization either.

Jacques Cartier and Samuel de Champlain

The Frenchman Jacques Cartier was the first one who *attempted* to establish a settlement. François I, the king of France, wished to continue Verrazano's voyages.

Consequently, in March 1534, he placed a considerable amount of money at Cartier's disposal to prepare the ships for exploration. The navigator completed three consecutive trips to Canada, namely in 1534, 1535 and 1541. The purpose of the trips was to locate new lands filled with riches and large quantities of gold.

And he reached his purpose, partly. He discovered Gaspe Bay – where he built a cross monument on behalf of the King of France, Chaleur Bay, Anticosti Island, Quebec City, Montreal. He was the first one that gave French names to Canadian places.

On his third expedition, Cartier came prepared with five ships and a crew comprising of 1,500 people. Nevertheless, the winter was harsh, and they dealt with scurvy and famine, which were commonly met at that time. As a result, they had to return to France. Even though the French explorer didn't succeed at establishing a French settlement in Canada, he gave France a claim to Canadian territory. In plain English, Jacques Cartier wasn't the one who discovered today's Canada, considering that he didn't reach New Brunswick, Prince

[31]

Edward Island, and Nova Scotia.

What he did discover was the *Canada River* and the St. Lawrence Valley. That being said, the name *Canada* was largely influenced by Jacques Cartier. Presumably, when he got acquainted with the Iroquois word for *town* or *village* – kana: ta, he decided to refer to the entire country in the same way. Additionally, Cartier's expeditions established the very first names of Canadian establishments.

From that point onward, the names of the places where either Amerindian or French. What is more, Cartier is known to have established the foundation for Canadian cartography. He uncovered the great seaway that provided New France three-quarters of the North American continent for a given timeframe.

From that point, French traders started to trade furs. Also, the Newfoundland, which was loaded with fish, became an important source of wealth for the French fleets. Apart from that, fleets from Spain, England, Portugal and the Basque country would consistently use the Grand Banks located off the coast of Newfoundland.

Jacques Cartier's expeditions were important in the sense that they established the stage for those of Samuel de Champlain and his descendants. Nevertheless, Cartier could be referred to as the father of French Canada, particularly in the St. Lawrence River Valley and Acadia. Still, another sixty years would pass until the French would become interested in what was due to become Canada.

Samuel de Champlain sailed a large part of the Atlantic seaboard; he reached Richelieu River. He also discovered the lake that presently bears his name. Additionally, he navigated Ottawa River, exploring the Great Lakes region, the country which, at that time, was known as Huronia.

In 1603, Champlain first sailed to New France as both a

cartographer and geographer. He is the acknowledged consolidator of the French Colonies in the New World, and the founder of the city of Quebec (1608).

It is assumed that Champlain was born as a commoner. Nevertheless, he worked hard to acquire a solid reputation as a navigator, after being part of the expeditions in Central America and the West Indies.

Champlain stood three consecutive years in Acadia. During the summers, he looked for the perfect spot for colonization. In 1608, Champlain attempted his most ambitious project, namely the founding of Quebec.

British Explorers

British explorers were also eager to find new routes towards Asia. On that note, Martin Frobisher set off on a journey in the 1570s. To be more precise, he completed three expeditions to the Canadian Arctic, in 1576, 1577 and 1578, north of Ungava Bay – Baffin Island. In fact, he was the very first European who traveled to what would later be known as Hudson Strait.

He investigated the southern coasts, and he reached Hudson Bay, right into James Bay. Whereas his discoveries appeared insignificant at that time, Frobisher played a crucial role. What he did was to open the passage for British travel to the Arctic regions. He came up with English names such as Cape Wolstenholme or Cape Digges.

Another noteworthy explorer was John Davis who started his voyage to the North Pole in 1585. The present-day map of the Polar Regions still carries the names of his friends, protectors, and ship-owners. Moreover, Canada's present-day Hudson Bay area soon became English territory, and the French didn't access it for a long time. That opened the path to an eventual English domination in Canada.

What is more, in 1615, William Baffin – British explorer – reached Hudson Strait and designed excellent navigational charts. During an upcoming expedition that took place in 1616, he would explore a segment of the bay that was named in his honor – Baffin Bay.

Humphrey Gilbert, another significant British explorer, left Plymouth for St. John, Newfoundland in 1583. At that point, he symbolically voiced *his possession* of the land on behalf of Queen Elizabeth I. In 1596, the Basques and Malouins (Bretons and Normans) were driven off the island. Even so, in the 1630s, a number of English did return in order to fish off the coasts. It's worth noting that, at that time, both Scottish and English fishers disheartened the efforts of colonizing the island.

Simply put, before the establishment of New France and Canada, both the French and the British were getting ready for the conquest of North America. The French had concentrated on exploring Newfoundland, as well as the valley and the Gulf of the St. Lawrence, while the British ventured towards the north.

The French, the British and the First Nations

The European settlers in Canada, who were mostly from France and Great Britain, progressively established networks of trading posts and small outposts. As the French and the British enlarged their colonies, each European power established affiliations with distinct First Nations groups. For example, the French were concerned about the lower population present in their colonial settlements. That's why they were keen to make allies.

Evidently, the alliances with the British and the French had decidedly influenced the life of the First Nations communities.

Eventually, France and Britain engaged in military conflict, and their allies were included in the battles, with or without their will. What is more, since Canada incorporated both British and French colonies, the wars that took place in Europe would further affect the political situation in Canada. An example would be the Treaty of Utrecht, at the end of the War of the Spanish Succession, which dramatically diminished the French power in Canada. What is more, according to the Treaty of Paris, the British Empire was provided with exclusive power in Canada.

In essence, these aspects altered the way in which First Nations communities collaborated with European colonists. That's because the French and the British could no longer fight their wars on Canadian soil.

Common Misconceptions about the European Exploration

1. North America Was A Peaceful Utopia before the Arrival of the White Man

At the moment, there are numerous misconceptions and myths concerning everything, including the history of North America and the colonization. One of these is that North America used to be a peaceful, perfect utopia before the Europeans set foot on American soil, which is far from being the truth.

According to historians, Native Americans engaged in military conflicts long before the coming of the Europeans. Records and archeological evidence outline one thing: throughout the American continent, there were diseases, conflict, and the typical elements that feature any other society.

We could have a look at numerous examples that indicate

signs of injustice between indigenous people in the North American continent. Still, we'll refer to the common ones.

The society in North America was, in essence, hierarchical, comprising of a noble class, a commoner class, and a slave class. It meets the specifications of the Old World perfectly. Another example would be what happened with the Iroquois in 1650, to put an end to their wars with the Wendats. The Wendats were named Hurons by the French. At that time, they were a Confederacy of 5 nations. It was similar to the Iroquois Confederacy, which is more acknowledged.

The Wendats established economic alliances with some of their neighbors. It is argued that they represented an advanced merchant nation, which was continually developing. They would produce corn, which was traded in exchange for tobacco, to the Petuns. The Wendats could be referred to as *the Swiss of North America*. Attacking them was off limits. As for the New France Company, it was also integrated into their economic alliances, being a partner like the others.

On the other hand, the Iroquois aimed at obtaining a large amount of weaponry, in order to attack their neighbors. As a result, the year of 1650 recorded a dreadful massacre. The Iroquois invaded the allies and abolished them. In fact, some historians argue that the Iroquois could be held liable for committing genocide.

This act was so upsetting that peace with the French became an unattainable purpose. The Iroquois had determined the downfall of the economic partners of the French, which determined the succession of the Franco-Iroquois wars from 1660 to 1701.

This is just an example indicating that North America wasn't perfect before the arrival of the Europeans. Still, this doesn't mean that the native Canadians didn't have numerous advantages. It just means that we shouldn't misinterpret history and assume things.

2. Europeans Didn't Benefit from North American Native Inventions

I'll refer to three significant inventions that the entire world has benefited from: namely the canoe, the umiak (skin boat) and the kayak. These small-sized native American boats represent some of the most practical and elegant watercraft. That's why they have been adopted throughout the world, in favor of local designs.

For starters, the canoe I'm referring to is the one that is pointed at each end, featuring nimble, rapid-shooting-wooden framed craft. Typically, in the manufacturing of such a canoe, a skin of birch bark, or other similar thin material is used. Many people are uninformed regarding the inventions that should be attributed to Native Americans. Most of the times, we hear about the fact that the Europeans have brought steel, or have introduced the wheel, but these significant inventions are overlooked.

The second one, the umiak, was created by the ancestors of the Intuit and Eskimo people in the North American Arctic. Essentially, it is made of animal skins that are stretched over a wooden frame. The umiak is similar to a canoe, to some extent, in the sense that it makes it suitable for traveling along coasts, as well as along rivers.

However, distinct from the bark canoe, a conventional umiak is, at times, propelled with a sail. One can row it with single paddles or pairs of oars.

And lastly, the kayak is an agile boat, which is made especially for hunting. This kind of boat is less likely to be sunk. Even if it is overturned by rough waters, a skillful kayaker could maneuver the boat.

Even though the materials that are utilized in the

manufacturing of these boats have been updated, the technology has remained unaltered, and it belongs to North Americans.

Interesting Facts!

- The primary reason why the Europeans went to North America was that the continent provided a wide range of resources. When they accidentally reached North America, they realized that the land was abundant with natural resources that included fur, minerals, animals, gold, and other metals. They concluded that building establishments there could bring financial advantages.
- Plundering the New World of its treasures was respectable because the land was populated by pagans. That being said, Christianizing the pagans was part of God's plan for the world, which gave the Europeans the right to conquer the territories of North America.
- The French Empire failed to compete with the wealth of New Spain and the growing expansion of the neighboring British colonies.

If the Choice Were Yours

- What would you have done if you were in the shoes of a European king at the time of the exploration of the New World? Would you have sent a team of explorers to discover new lands or would you have acted otherwise?

Chapter 4 - British and French Colonization and Decolonization

After the discoveries of Martin Frobisher, Giovanni Caboto, Humphrey Gilbert, and others, England moved its attention towards the New World. In 1607, it institutionalized the first overseas colony, known as Virginia (New England) – which was named to honor Queen Elizabeth I, referred to as *Virgin Queen*.

In 1583, Sir Humphrey Gilbert reached the harbor of St. John's, Newfoundland. His attempt to claim land in the name of the Queen failed, at that time. Still, the attempt was primarily propelled by England's wish to expand its control over the fish trade.

The Company of New France

From the early 16th century, France was a major colonial power in North America. The French presence in North America was featured by economic exchanges with Aboriginal peoples, as well as conflicts since the French attempted to control the Canadian territory. The French colonial enterprise was also prompted by religious motivation, as well as the objective of setting up an efficient colony in the St. Lawrence Valley.

The French government furnished active support after the remarkable revival of royal power. That was accomplished by Armand-Jean du Plessis, cardinal et duc de Richelieu in the 1620s. Richelieu aimed at creating a French colony that would compare to that of the Netherlands or England.

Richelieu used his resources in order to create the Company of New France, also referred to as the Hundred Associates. Its main objective was to exploit new resources and establish new lands of New France. The company enjoyed high responsibility and far-reaching power, as follows: the monopoly of trade with all New France, Acadia and Canada, the obligation of taking out 400 settlers a year, powers of government, and keeping the Roman Catholic faith in New France.

The company was chartered, and, in 1627, its capital was raised. Notwithstanding, the upcoming year, war broke out with the British. They would support the French Protestants, also known as Huguenots, who were fighting against Richelieu. The conflict wasn't handled accordingly, and things were left up in the air. As a result, English adventurers – the Kirke brothers blockaded St. Lawrence in 1628 – managed to capture Quebec in 1629. For three years' time, the Kirkes and their French associates were in charge of the fur trade. That took Champlain by surprise, who had been taken prisoner to England.

It is challenging to pinpoint the effect that the war had on the Hundred Associates. In 1632, though, Acadia and Canada were restored by the Treaty of Saint German-en-Laye. In the following year, namely in 1632, the company retook possession. At first sight, everything seemed to function excellently. Champlain regained his position as governor, the Jesuits have taken full responsibility for Roman Catholicism in Canada, and the fur trade was resumed.

The company would remain in charge of New France until 1663, offering a sequence of governors and officials. Notwithstanding, it wasn't capable of colonizing. Exhausted by its profitless tasks, the company leased the fur trade to other businesses. In 1645, the fur trade had been leased to a group of Canadian residents referred to as the Community of Habitats.

The Character of the French Settlement

It is fundamental to comprehend that fur trade wasn't the only enterprise in New France. Actually, by 1645, Canadian settlers provided provisions for the annual ships and fur traders. A typical mode of landholding, referred to as the seigniorial system, started to develop.

This system implied that the state offered parcels of land to seigneurs, who were afterward liable for securing habitats. Additionally, they had the responsibility to facilitate essential services such as a road to the nearest town, a mill, so on and so forth.

In other words, the inhabitants were offered large plots of approximately 100 acres (40 hectares) and were obligated to pay dues. The system was similar to the semi-feudal seigniorial system in France.

Notwithstanding, three elements made the system less feudal and more flexible than it was in France. In New France, the district military leader was the local militia captain, as opposed to the seigneur. Secondly, the seigneur didn't enjoy a political distinction that would differentiate him from the rest of the inhabitants. Due to the abundance of available land, the seigneur was less likely to exercise a genuine semi-feudal discipline on the inhabitants. And lastly, the inhabitants would eventually end up possessing the plots, having the right to give them to their children.

The missionary endeavor of the Jesuits was, at times, an excellent partner or a rival of the fur trade. The Jesuits had two obligations. Firstly, they had to keep New France Catholic by excluding the Huguenots and ministering to its people. And secondly, they had to convert the native Canadians. They learned the native languages in an attempt to determine the natives to convert to the Christian faith. Still, the missionaries succeeded in converting very few Aboriginal persons. Additionally, they transmitted a wide range of European diseases. Regrettably, the natives had no resistance against those illnesses, which led to massive numbers of deaths.

In this respect, the Huron would comprehend that, as opposed to the warnings voiced by the missionaries, God's wrath didn't crash down on them due to their ungodliness. On the contrary, the coming of the missionaries was the source of the problems. During the 1630s, measles and smallpox annihilated the Huron population, leading to the death of thousands. Furthermore, by the 1640s, the population was reduced to half. In spite of the missionaries' efforts to treat those conditions, numerous allied tribes suffered the same fate.

What is more, a range of military and political events diminished the efficacy of France's colonization efforts. To be more precise, the alliances established by Champlain eventually made enemies among the Iroquois. The Iroquois nations eventually became quarrelsome, which led to the Iroquois wars. The sequence of attacks at the core of the colony reduced the colony's chances of survival.

In 1663, Quebec would be a commercial branch operation. The fur trade was in opposition to the agriculture branch. What is more, the French population was quite small. And on top of all that, the administration of the colony by the commercial exploiters wasn't that fruitful. On that note, the company surrendered the control and governing of the colony to the king.

Royal Rule Maximizes Development

Under the governance of Louis XIV, New France was made a province belonging to France, and it prospered. The hierarchical administrative organization was similar to

France's.

It's important to highlight that the first twenty years of King Louis XIV's reign were the most flourishing of them all. His ministers – Colbert and the Marquis de Louvois – ensured an optimal administrative and financial reorganization of the kingdom. Additionally, he focused on the development of manufacturing and trade. He also restored the army, as a result enjoying numerous military victories that facilitated the flourishing of the French culture.

Under the rule of marquis de Tracy, Carignan-Salières Regiment constructed powerful forts, destroyed Iroquois villages and proved French military power. As a result, the Iroquois made peace, and approximately 400 soldiers stayed in the colony as settlers. Apart from that, the king had sent 850 young women, as brides-to-be. In other words, he encouraged the formation of families, which would afterward facilitate the development of the colony.

Approximately 20 years later, the demographic situation was entirely different. In 1663, there was a woman to every six men. Nevertheless, after twenty years, the sexes were roughly equal in numbers. On that note, the colony had *refreshed* 90 percent of its numbers through childbirth.

Exploration and Economic Expansion

The pacification of the Iroquois and the necessity for rebuilding the network of fur-trade treaties contributed to the explorations in the Great Lakes and Mississippi regions. These explorations were led by important people such as Louis Jolliet, Francois Dollier de Casson, Jacques Marquette, and the Cavelier de La Salle.

Notwithstanding, the Iroquois Wars had begun again in 1682, which highlighted the need for the involvement of new heroes, such as Pierre Le Moyne d'Iberville. Economic factors associated with missionary and military activity outlined the need for furs to be purchased from Aboriginal peoples.

Taking advantage of the partly favorable circumstances, Jean Talbot initiated a dynamic development program. Apart from managing the agriculture and fur trade, Talon commenced ventures such as trade with the West Indies, shipbuilding, fishing industries, commercial crops like hemp and flax, and he also constructed a brewery. Still, in 1672, the economic circumstances had altered dramatically, and nothing remained of these beneficial initiatives.

It could be challenging to pinpoint the fundamental elements of this commencing society. Still, in the case of Acadia, the most important features were the significance of fishing, the quality of the agricultural establishments and the alternating French and British regimes. As for St. Lawrence Valley, farmers were clearing the land. In the meantime, artisans didn't enjoy the support of big enterprises. Fur traders were coping with unfortunate economic situations and burdensome regulations, although they facilitated the colony's exports.

The Start of the Economic Crisis

New France attained its maximum territorial extent at the beginning of the 18th century. Approximately 250 people would live in almost a dozen settlements in Newfoundland. In Acadia, there were about 1,500. Around the Great Lakes and Mississippi, there were also several hundred. That being said, Canada encompassed nearly 20,000 inhabitants. Most of them were farmers that lived between the two urban centers of Montreal and Quebec.

Still, irrespective of the expansion, New France was portrayed as a *colossus with feet of clay*. On the other hand, the British

American colonies were 20 times as populous. We will expand more on the conflict between the French and British rule in Canada throughout this chapter.

English Colonization of Newfoundland

England's upcoming colonization move started in 1610 in Newfoundland, namely at Anse-à-Cuper. John Guy, English explorer, colonized Conception Bay, which was situated on the northwest of the Avalon Peninsula. English, Spanish, French, and Portuguese fishers had been living on the island for approximately a century.

The Newfoundland Colonization Company was owned by Sir Francis Bacon, and John Guy actually acted on his behalf. In time, St John's city developed, the fishing trade became more and more profitable, and various English Merchants settled on the harbor.

Sir David Kirke was granted rights to the English segment of the island, in 1638. Nevertheless, the French argued the British occupation.

In 1662, the French renounced St. John's for Plaisance, which would later become Newfoundland's French capital. In the meantime, St. John's was recognized as English capital. At that time, approximately 1,700 people dwelt on the English coast, between Trepassey and Bonavista.

These merchants and fishermen originated primarily from southeastern Ireland and southwestern England. They spoke Irish or regional English. They were commissioned to stay since the British authorities feared that the French could take control over the most profitable fishing harbors.

The primary governor of the Queen was appointed in 1729 – which was sixteen years after the Treaty of Utrecht that gave

Great Britain control of the island.

By the end of the 18th century, Newfoundland's population was of 20,000 people; they spoke English. By 1815, the population doubled to 40,000. Nevertheless, it was only in 1817 that the English governor started dwelling on the island.

As mercantilism commanded provincial politics, British merchants were long able to deter the development of a major colony. They kept control of the harbors and fishing ports, while the island was, for the most part, a naval base visited by fishing boats. On that note, the French language didn't disappear, since France kept its rights to seasonal fishing on the *French Shore*. Also, it acquired the small archipelago of Saint-Pierre-et-Miquelon in 1763, which remained an important site for fishing on the Grand Banks.

Rupert's Land and the Hudson's Bay Company

Moving on to the Hudson Bay area, King Charles II of England had singed a charter. That happened on 2nd May 1670, when the Hudson's Bay Company was founded. It was also known as the *Governor and Company of Adventurers of England Trading for Hudson's Bay*.

The ones that established the oldest trade company that operates until today were two Canadian fur traders. I'm referring to Pierre-Esprit Radisson and Médard Chouart des Groseilliers. Since the French colonial government didn't offer the two explorers a permit, they provided their services to the English crown instead, in this way initiating a trading post on the northwest border of New France.

The King of England granted the Hudson's Bay Company absolute right to trade in the far-reaching territory. He also named Rupert's Land on behalf of Prince Rupert, who was one of the company managers and also the king's cousin. Rupert's Land included 7.7 million square kilometers, as well as the entire Hudson's Bay watershed. To be more precise, Rupert's Land would cover a significant portion of Canada's present-day territory, namely the Northwest Territories, Manitoba, and Nunavut.

In the meantime, the Hudson's Bay Company wasn't interested in establishing colonies as the French had in the St. Lawrence River Valley or Acadia. The British were focused entirely on the fur trade. At the mouths of the most important rivers, they constructed small wood forts. These facilitated the natives to travel by canoe to trade their beaver skins. Gradually, the language of communication between the natives and the whites would become English. As for trading posts and rivers, they were given English names as well.

In essence, the British colonization of Canada evolved slowly and steadily. It started with the fishing ports in Newfoundland and Acadia, and it followed with the establishment of a range of trading posts in the proximity of Hudson Bay.

Additionally, the English Colonization was deep rooted in the South, in New England. By 1663, Canada's population was of 3,500, whereas that of Acadia's was of 400. In New England, there were about 70,000 inhabitants.

The Treaty of Utrecht (1713)

The Treaty of Utrecht represented a treaty between France and other European Powers. This treaty ended the 1704-1714 War of the Spanish Succession between a coalition of France, Spain, some German and Italian principalities and the Grand Alliance. The Grand Alliance included England, the German-Roman Empire, the United Provinces, and Portugal and Savoy – which joined later on.

[47]

In order to obtain peace, Louis XIV had to renounce the colonies. For the most part, the agreements were in favor of England – which in 1701 had officially become Great Britain. As a result, Newfoundland was transferred to the British. Nevertheless, French fishermen had kept their right to fish on the north shore of the island, namely between Cape Bonavista and Pointe Riche, which was later referred to as the French Shore, or the Treaty Coast.

What is more, France had to acknowledge Great Britain's domination over the land of the Iroquois Confederacy. It is needless to say that this offended the Iroquois greatly, who thought that the two European powers weren't entitled to decide their fate. Irrespective of that, the map of North America had been inevitably changed.

In plain English, the Treaty of Utrecht was a massive struck for France in North America. However, the country received some restitution that would compensate its loss. Great Britain received Newfoundland, but the French fishermen kept their rights to fish and dry their catch on the shore of the island.

Plus, although France had to renounce continental Acadia (Nova Scotia), it kept controlling Cape Breton Island, and St. John's Island. Furthermore, France established a new colony on Cape Breton Island and constructed the renowned fortress of Louisburg.

Still, a segment of continental Acadia, which accounts for present-day New Brunswick, would be a *disputed territory* between the French and the British. That's because each of the European powers interpreted the situation subjectively.

Under British rule, the Acadians of Nova Scotia enjoyed living in peace, except for a few incidents determined by English colonists. Additionally, English colonists repopulated the island of Newfoundland. Most of the colonists were brought from western England, even though the Irish Catholics had their Irish traditions. Afterward, the forts captured by the French in Hudson Bay area were occupied by the English.

During this timeframe, a succession of British-French conflicts had been monitored. As a result, the names for various forts had been changed. In plain English, the 1713 Treaty of Utrecht was the starting point for the Treaty of Paris in 1763, which diminished the French presence in North America.

French-British Rivalry in North America

At the beginning of the 17th century, both France and England had established colonies in North America, Africa, the East and West Indies. They established a range of profitable monopolies, primarily slaves from Africa, sugar from the West Indies, spices and silk from the East Indies, and fish and furs from North America.

In 1628, hostilities started to take place in the New World, and they persisted unrelenting until 1762. Notwithstanding, the root of the French-English conflict began in Europe when England wanted to minify Louis XIV's expansionist aspirations. It ended with Napoleon's defeat at Waterloo.

What is more, the conflict developed into a series of consecutive maritime wars between the two European countries as both aimed at enlarging their empires at the expense of the other. It goes without saying that the existence of this ongoing conflict affected the way in which the French and English expanded around the world. Evidently, the rivalry broadened in North America, as well, where both European powers had established colonies.

The Treaty of Paris (1763) and North America

The Treaty of Paris from 1763 ceased the Seven Years' War (1756-1763) between Great Britain and France. Additionally, New France, apart from Louisiana, was possessed by the British. As for France, it occupied the small islands of Saint-Pierre-et-Miquelon, which were located south of Newfoundland. Meanwhile, the Spanish have come to possess Louisiana.

The Seven Years' War was truly disastrous for France. France had to renounce its territorial holdings in North America, transferring them to Great Britain. Still, France retained its rights in the Gulf of St. Lawrence and Newfoundland. What is more, in lines with the conditional capitulation of 1760, Great Britain guaranteed French Canadians the freedom to worship according to their religion. Additionally, the French had 18 months at their disposal to immigrate if they wished to do so.

Simply put, the British colonists didn't have to worry about the ongoing threat of the French presence on Canadian territory. What is more, the additional territory the British had gained after the treaty enabled the empire to expand to the west.

On the other hand, France's military dignity had diminished considerably, its finances were ruined, and its maritime power was severely weakened. The loss of New France is conveyed as the most considerable French defeat of all times, in contrast with Napoleon's defeats that seem negligible.

On the other hand, the Treaty of Paris confirmed Great Britain's position as the greatest empire in the entire world and that North America would be English. Oddly enough, the word Canada was no longer used in official documents from that point onward, since Great Britain wanted to erase the country's ties with France.

What about the influence the treaty had on the native peoples? In the course of time, the Treaty of Paris created a significant friction between the American colonies and the government of Great Britain. With the withdrawal of the French from North America, the British diminished the military presence on the continent, as it involved large expenses. In the meantime, the introduction of levy taxes on the colonies represented Great Britain's attempt to acquire finances in order to pay for the debts accumulated during the war.

On a final note, Britain would eventually lose the southern North American colonies in the American Revolution, and the northern country would, later on, become the modern country of Canada.

The American Revolution (1775 – 1783)

The American Revolution was an act of rebellion against colonial authorities, a revolt against the King of England – George the 3rd – and the monarchical regime. In technical terms, it was a war of *national liberation* – the first one recorded in modern history. It is acknowledged as one of the bloodiest wars pursued by the United States (after the Civil War).

It goes without saying that the American Revolution had noteworthy consequences in British North America. The *Constitutional Act of 1791* and the Québec Act of 1774 were linked to the American Revolution.

Not only that it changed the Canadian-American border, which significantly diminished British holdings, but it also altered the demographic element of Canada, as a considerable number of British loyalists had come from the American colonies. Furthermore, these changes determined the establishment of another *province* or British colony, namely

New Brunswick, and the separation of Quebec into two distinct colonies: Upper Canada (Ontario) and Lower Canada (Quebec).

At the start of the American Revolution, namely in 1775, Canada was invaded by rebel forces that occupied Montreal and attacked the town of Quebec. What is more, American privateers also attacked Atlantic ports. Nova Scotia had revolutionary sympathizers, who actually attempted at initiating a rebellion in that colony. Even though Canada eventually defeated the rebel forces, the 13 American colonies earned their independence from Britain, leading to a distinct kind of invasion, namely a wave of Loyalist immigration that would eventually alter the make-up of Canada.

The arrival of loyalists diversified the composition of the population of British North American companies by incorporating American elements. Plus, the coming of the loyalists also increased the population by 6,000 in Quebec. Apart from these, there were also important numbers of *late loyalists,* who were essentially land seekers who reached the northern states as late as 1812. Approximately 80,000 came to Nova Scotia. Nevertheless, not all remained there. About 20,000 decided to settle in New Brunswick and a couple of hundreds on Prince Edward Island.

It's important to note that not all American colonists were adepts of the independence cause, and many chose to resist it. Due to the hostilities that took place eventually, the loyalists were required to make peace with the new republic, which is why numerous chose to go into exile. The refugees referred to as United Empire Loyalists, raised a number of concerns for the British government, as it wanted to compensate for their losses and to aid them in finding new homes. As a result, some went to the British West Indies, others went to the British Empire, but most of them emigrated to Quebec or Nova Scotia.

In Quebec, the loyalists crossed the frontier and chose to settle along the St. Lawrence River. The effect that this fact had on Quebec was evidently more noteworthy than it was in Nova Scotia, as it determined the creation of the Constitutional Act of 1791. What did it imply? The Constitutional Act, also referred to as the Canada Act, was a response to the British Parliament that revoked certain portions of the Quebec Act of 1774. It created a new constitution for the two colonies, as the territory was divided into halves: Lower Canada (the future Quebec) and Upper Canada (the future Ontario).

The newcomers had influenced the society in the sense that they further diversified the colonies. For example, in Newfoundland, there was a growing number of Irish inhabitants. As for Nova Scotia, it was occupied by loyalists, New Englanders, Yorkshire men, the Highland Scots of Pictou, and the Germans of Lunenburg. In 1806, New Brunswick's population was about 35,000. In Upper Canada, there were about 70,718, and in Lower Canada, there were approximately 250,000.

In this respect, these were the nations that would create the first Canadian population mosaic, representing a blend of British, French, and German. Evidently, the British element would be strengthened by northern English, Lowland and Highland Scots, and northern and southern Irish. This blend resulted in the establishment of a society in which religious liberty and social equality were mandatory for social cohesion.

Notwithstanding, until 1815, the number of immigrants was still growing. Only after 1830 did Canada see a notable population growth. That happened due to the coming of Irish, British and Scottish to the British North America in significant volume. Therein, every year, thousands would arrive. The primary element that attracted so many immigrants to North America was freedom of religion.

The British North American colonies consisted of British inhabitants, primarily, with the exception of Lower Canada.

That is something that would influence the course of Canadian history for the next century.

Decolonization

Decolonization represents the process through which colonies accomplish their independence from the colonizing country. Decolonization is typically a lengthy process, which involves reassessing the values and principles of the aboriginal peoples and acquiring the status of independence.

Canada's conversion from a self-governing British colony into an entirely independent state was a developmental process. That being said, it would be difficult to indicate an exact date. Notwithstanding, there are some crucial episodes that have played a fundamental role in this respect.

One of these episodes is the war of 1812, which could be traced to the U.S. – Anglo rivalry for the fur trade. The War of 1812 was a conflict between Great Britain and the United States, which occurred as a result of the British violation of U.S. maritime rights. The tensions that eventually led to the war emerged due to the French Revolutionary and Napoleonic Wars (1792 – 1815). During the ongoing conflict between Britain and France, the American interests were severely damaged by the countries' efforts in preventing the United States from trading with one another.

In the long run, the war was ended with no compromise on either side. Nevertheless, it managed to push back the Indian frontier, while maximizing the rupture between the British North American colonies and the United States. What is more, the war validated the U.S. – Canadian border, as both the French and British had united their powers and fought against the U.S. invasion.

Other episodes worth mentioning would be the Rebellions of

1837-1838. Immediately after the War of 1812, political unrest developed in both Lower and Upper Canada. The primary reason was the governing structure that was enforced by the 1791 Constitution. In the meantime, other causes developed due to each colony's distinctive elements. In both colonies, the rise of the middle class would play a significant role in the Rebellions. The middle class comprised primarily of journalists and lawyers.

However, the unsuccessful rebellious actions highlighted the urgency to reform Canada's restrictive and outdated constitution. Hence, by 1855, the British North American colonies accomplished self-government, and their institutions and laws were reassessed in order to meet the individual specifications of each colony. One of the most crucial steps made towards the union was the creation of the Great Coalition, a government that united the leaders from Canada West and Canada East.

In 1867, Canada's status as a colony was determined by legal and political subjugation to the British Empire in all governmental aspects: executive, judicial and legislative. The ultimate executive power was anchored in the British Monarch, who was assisted by British ministers only in its exercise.

What is highly remarkable about the gradual process of decolonization is that it was accomplished through minimum legislative amendments. In short, it could be argued that Canada gained its independence by developing new political arrangements, some of which had been turned into judicial decisions that interpreted the Constitution.

Canada's passing from being an indispensable component of the British Empire to becoming an independent member of the Commonwealth accurately highlights the manner in which quintessential constitutional rules have matured, over time.

[55]

On the 1st of July, 1867, Queen Victoria gave an official decree that granted Canada the right to cope with its internal affairs via the British North America Act. Therein, Canada was established as a Domination of Great Britain. It gained its full independence in 1931 when Great Britain provided its dominions full autonomy.

Common Misconceptions about Canada's Colonization and Decolonization

1. Before Colonization, North America Was Pristine and Untouched

Many individuals indicate that the Europeans are to be blamed for destroying the natural landscapes of North America. Evidently, one of the fundamental motivations for colonization was the abundance of natural resources that could be found on the North American territory. Nevertheless, that doesn't imply that, before the colonization took place, the land was pristine and untouched. This idea was actually devised by writers that were pining for the past. The idealization of the past isn't a new thing, apparently.

That being said, these writers affirmed that the depopulation was translated in natural habitat degeneration. Still, before the arrival of the Europeans, the North American landscape wasn't as untouched. Irrespective of the popular imagery that indicates how the Aboriginal peoples respected the natural world when the Europeans reached North America, they found a landscape that was changed in order to meet the population's farming and hunting needs.

In truth, the forests in North America had been turned into meadows, or open fields, which would be controlled by burning. According to early colonists, the remaining forests were far from being lush. On the opposite, they were replaced by grassy wide pathways and openings among the trees. Apparently, the layout of the forests was the result of attentively planned fires set by the aboriginal peoples.

2. Everyone Enjoyed Religious Tolerance in North America

This affirmation is accurate, to some extent. It is true that one of the elements that feature the Canadian nation is religious tolerance. Nevertheless, colonization had other motivations, apart from the desire to acquire wealth and land.

The Europeans strongly believed that they had a holy mission of converting the pagans that inhabited North America. In fact, they thought they were entitled to get their land because they were Christians and the aboriginal peoples were pagans.

What is more, the New France Company actually brought numerous missionaries that aimed at converting the indigenous to Christianity. In spite of their efforts, though, they didn't manage to convert considerable numbers of people.

That being said, in the early phase of the colonization, religious tolerance wasn't that representative of Canada. This had become a crucial feature in the next centuries, with the coming of the loyalists and other emigrants.

Interesting Facts!

- The name *Canada* stands for a linguistic error. Jacques Cartier, important French explorer, misunderstood the way in which the natives referred to their country. When he first visited the New World, the indigenous people invited him to their village. The word for a village in their language was *Kanata*. Cartier thought that they referred to the entire country, and he thought they said *Canada*.

- King Louis XIV had ended the period of religious tolerance in France, as he revoked the Edict of Nantes in 1685. That led to the expulsion of French Protestants from France.
- In the post-Confederation era, until the end of the First World War, Great Britain represented Canada's primary fundamental trading and investment partner. Only at the beginning of the 1920s did the trade with the US surpass the trade with Great Britain. Before the First World War, the trade between the US and Canada was small and still developing.
- The Second World War contributed to the development of Canada into an important North American economy. The military conflict contributed to the growing US interest in Canada's natural resources, including oil and gas.
- Canada has depended on foreign capital for evolving since the Confederation. Without it, the economy is thought to have been underdeveloped and the living standards much lower.

If the Choice Were Yours

- If you were in King Louis XIV's shoes, would you have done anything else differently, in order to secure New France's prosperity for an extended time frame?

Chapter 5 - Canada's Influence in the World Today

Modern-day Canada is acknowledged for its interest in preserving human rights, fostering tolerance and multiculturalism.

The ongoing debate regarding Canada's role and influence in the world isn't new. Nevertheless, this aspect is much more important considering the context of global power shifts, and the ever-growing competition among states for expanding influence, access, and prosperity.

Aiming at comprehending Canada's place in the world necessitates an appraisal of various factors and dimensions.

Simply put, a country's influence in the international context is largely assessed by its military power, economic situation, and diplomacy and development assistance. That being said, the Canadian economy is acknowledged as being the ninth largest on a global scale. So, it has dealt with the financial crisis that started in 2008 surprisingly well.

Similar to other advanced economies that take advantage of foreign and trade investment, Canada has to ensure that its domestic conditions are adequate as in to facilitate its international commercial competitiveness. On that note, there is a stressing need to improve two crucial areas, namely innovation and productivity.

Furthermore, Canada's military force, encompassing approximately 70,000 personnel plus 24,000 reservists is esteemed among its allies. That being said, a few years ago, the Canadian Forces made their contribution to the international mission in Afghanistan and other important operations in Libya and Haiti.

The anti-piracy maritime efforts in Africa are also noteworthy in this respect. Concurrently, Canada's distribution to the United Nations peacekeeping missions has diminished over the decades. That being said, Canada occupies the 51st place among the countries that contributed to these missions.

The Department of Foreign Affairs and International Trade (DFAIT) is liable for promoting diplomacy, which, for ongoing years, has been the primary element that defined and illustrated Canada's foreign policy. As a result of notable changes that took place given the context of globalization, more than 20 federal government agencies and departments are internationally active.

At the same time, numerous central agencies aim at actively participating in coordinating Canada's international policies. It's also worth noting that the DFAIT's external approach has concentrated on constructing coherence across Canada's diplomatic attempts in distinct policy areas.

Canada's Part in Global Environmental Issues

Canada has a vision in encouraging people to make responsible choices regarding the environment. On that note, it actively collaborates with other countries to ensure a thriving, clean planet for everyone.

So, Canada is part of a range of important environmental organizations such as The Organization of American States (OAS), the Organization for Economic Cooperation and Development (OECD), and the Asia-Pacific Economic Cooperation (APEC). So, it could be said that Canada plays a crucial part on an international stage, contributing to accomplishing global results when it comes to preserving the environment.

Additionally, Canada is currently actively involved in the global environmental protection movement. In this direction, it signed bilateral agreements with 18 countries that cope with various issues. Some of them are the Watershed Management (Canada-Brazil), or Technological and Scientific Cooperation (Canada-Japan). Furthermore, there are 19 multilateral agreements as well, which address other crucial environmental problems such as the conservation of polar bears.

Canada Could Be Conveyed as an Internationally Engaged Country

Canada *could* play a fundamental role in the world. Nevertheless, the last years have noted a decline in the international importance in peacemaking and other crucial international security activities.

According to historians, Canada is thought to have begun the post-Cold War period strong, having skilled diplomatic corps and a renowned foreign minister that was engaged in international affairs and was eager to take risks.

What is more, most experts that voiced their opinion regarding Canada outlined its courageous position in supporting majority rule in South Africa and Namibia.

Additionally, Canada played a crucial role in establishing the foundations for global and regional trade agreements (WTO and NAFTA). In essence, Canada did a good job at combining economic integration with political independence. Foreign observers perceived Canada as being efficient in constructing and maintaining strong relationships with the US. Mulroney has pursued the most important Canadian interests in bilateral negotiations.

Moreover, Canada constructed long-lasting relationships with the UK and France. Also, many external observers point that

Canada has played an important role in numerous aspects of the human security agenda, such as the Criminal Court, child soldiers, and others.

When it comes to Canada's relationship with the US, it is crucial to differentiate between their roles as neighbors and international interlocutors. For Canada to play a major role in the US foreign policy formation, two questions ought to be answered: *what is Canada's viewpoint of the US? What valuable assets can Canada bring?*

Truth be told, a country's military power is one of its primary assets. Unfortunately, Canada's defense assets are lacking considering the international security needs. As for UN peacemaking, Canada's part in the equation is insignificant.

Improving its military effectiveness could be one of the steps that Canada should take. The Canadian military has been involved almost entirely in disaster relief or peacemaking, both on international and on a national scale, during the last four decades of the twentieth century.

That being said, Canada has contributed to offering conflict forces collective war efforts during this timeframe. Nevertheless, the engagements have been quite small. As of 2001, the military force experienced reorganization and restructuring. As a result, the role that Canada's military force will play in the future remains uncertain.

Canada should also make a contribution to international security. Foreign observers indicate that, with the right military assets and political approach, Canada could make a significant addition to international security. Refocusing the military assets could mean improving security and making an *actual* difference abroad.

From a historical mindset, Canada has had a leadership role in development cooperation. Nevertheless, at the moment, it has lost that position, in comparison with other countries.

A question imminently follows: *how could Canada make a difference?* By having the right political support and leadership, Canada is capable of establishing a unique leadership position in the international context. Also, Canada could play a significant role in peace enforcement. Thirdly, Canada is conveyed as one of the most important global centers of education. As a result, this is a significant source of economic growth that should be exploited.

In truth, Canada has fought for peace since it joined the UN. Its primary peacemaking mission was completed in 1949, in Pakistan and India. This is one of the aspects that portray the core of the Canadian identity and what it *could* be capable of doing.

Misconceptions about Canada's Influence in the World Today

1. Canada's International Status Is Insignificant

A widespread misconception regarding Canada's place in the world is the assumption that the world could definitely do without it. Due to Canada's vast size, being the second largest country after Russia, it provides an abundance of natural resources ranging from oil, uranium, lumber, electricity, and grains, which are exported worldwide. An important part of Canadian exports is directed towards the US, which is Canada's primary trading partner.

What is more, Canada's automotive and aerospace sector accounts for a major player in the international market. Still, Canada's most significant contribution to the world is presumably the role it plays in peace keeping. Simply put, Canadian officers had provided protection and assistance to some of the world's most troubled areas. While Canada's international position is far from being insignificant, it's true

[63]

that it could maximize its importance by taking advantage of its resources.

2. Immigrants Don't Contribute to Canada's development

During 1995 and 2005, nearly 25 percent of the high-tech companies based in Canada and America had been founded by immigrants. What is more, the companies that have been established by immigrants have loomed. Furthermore, even though immigrants account for less than 20 percent of the Canadian population, they possess half of new doctorate degrees in engineering, more precisely 45 percent of master's degrees in information technology and computer science.

That being said, the waves of immigrants are just as productive and ambitious as the previous waves of immigrants that have contributed to the establishment of a powerful nation that Canada has grown to become. That being said, diminishing the immigration levels could dramatically harm the economy and the future growth in numerous sectors, contrary to this misconception.

The noteworthy economic benefits provided by immigrants override the costs. Not to mention that Canada is gaining a notable advantage over other countries.

Interesting Facts!

- The Canada-US merchandise trade is acknowledged as the largest bilateral trading relationship in the world, reaching a total of $750.7 billion in 2014. Approximately 75.7 percent of Canada's total merchandise exports from 2014 went to the US, which was the equivalent of 20 percent of the Gross Domestic Product.

- The US represents the largest source of direct investment and debt capital in Canada.
- Quebec produces no less than two-thirds of the world's total of maple syrup.

If the Choice Were Yours

- What is your mindset regarding Canada's position and role in the international context? What would you do to maximize its political importance and what are the main elements you could consider before making a decision?

Chapter 6 - Canadian Culture

One cannot say that Canada incorporates a single culture. On the opposite, this country features a blend of cultures, each equally valued and significant. All of them have played a major role in shaping this great nation. Their values and ways of living have been extracted from various cultures and were incorporated over time.

In 1951, a report, which was later known as the Massey Report, was issued by the Royal Commission on National Development in the Arts, Letters and Sciences, indicating that Canadian culture has been dramatically diluted, being nearly indistinguishable from that of their neighboring country – the United States.

It could be argued that Canadian culture is a specific blend of French, British and American influences. Each of these has played a considerable role in shaping its culture.

I'm referring to all aspects, including film-making, sports, cooking – you get the picture. Additionally, other nations living on Canadian territory have also contributed to their culture. 20 years after the release of the Massey Report, Canada embraced multiculturalism as its national policy. Consequently, the federal government provides support to a range of ethnic groups so that they can have a role in the Canadian society.

Social Customs and Daily Life

Since Canada is so diverse from an ethnical and historical point of view, we cannot distinguish a singular national culture. On the opposite, we could say that Canadian culture is a mix representing distinct elements. Even though both English and French languages are acknowledged as being official, the culture of an area is typically illustrated in the language that dominates that area.

That being said, it is worth noting that French influences are particularly noteworthy in New Brunswick and Quebec. Canada's aboriginal peoples have preserved their cultures, as well, especially in the North. Plus, immigrants have integrated a range of typical elements of their ancestral homelands in their everyday lives.

We could also say that American and British influences are notably felt in the Canadian daily life especially in the English-speaking segments of the country. Presumably, Quebec's French culture is evident through its distinguishable architecture, cuisine, and music.

An example would be that there are a bunch of dishes that are especially popular in those areas. For instance, *poutine,* which are French fries topped with gravy and cheese and other unique dishes aren't present in other parts of the country.

Until recently, Canada's native people had been disgraced and located on the periphery of national society. That's why alcohol and drug addiction was overly widespread in certain reserves.

Nevertheless, recently, Canada aimed at recapturing their traditions. Nowadays, Indian art, such as bone or stone sculpture, carving or basket-making are quite popular.

In truth, it could be said that the arts and crafts illustrate specific features that classify and characterize the region.

Multiculturalism in Canada

Multiculturalism, as a concept, has emerged in Canada in the 1960s, to counteract *biculturalism,* which was promoted by

[67]

the *Royal Commission on Bilingualism and Biculturalism*. It has substituted the notion *cultural pluralism* almost entirely; nevertheless, that term is still utilized in Quebec.

A considerably debatable concept, multiculturalism has been used in three distinct senses:

- to invoke a society that is featured by cultural or ethnic heterogeneity
- to address an ideal of mutual respect and equality among a population's cultural groups
- lastly, multiculturalism has referred to the policies incorporated by the federal government in 1971

That being said, this concept is conveyed as being an integral element of Canada's identity at many levels. Historians and sociologists assert that individual ethnicity doesn't substitute the Canadian identity; on the opposite: it defines Canada and its place in the world.

Immigration Linked to Multiculturalism

The arrival of the British explorers at the beginning of the 15th century and the French and British colonization has made Canada become one of the most significant immigrant-receiving societies. As a matter of fact, it preserved this status through the 1920s and after the World War Two. In Anglophone regions, immigrants were predicted to fit in the English majority. As in Quebec, most immigrants that arrived during this time frame arrived in Montreal, when some learned both French and English.

This prediction of cultural assimilation was encompassed in the concept of the *melting pot*. This is a term that has grown in popularity in both Canada and the US, after the production of the play with the same name, in 1908. The play mirrored the incorporation of a Russian Jewish man into American culture.

In Canada, the considerable primary challenge to the melting pot scenario emerged in 1938, after John Murray Gibbon published *Canadian Mosaic: The Making of a Northern Nation*. This book argued that Canada could *actually* take advantage of the cultural diversity of its ethnic groups. From that point onward, the class privilege relished by British people began being criticized, just as the marginalization of other cultural groups.

It was at that time that Canada started to welcome the ever-growing number of non-white immigrants. In the 1960s, former policies regarding racial discrimination in the immigration system were declared null.

Additionally, in 1971, for the very first time, most of the new immigrants didn't originate from European countries. That's a paradigm that has endured ever since. In this direction, the 2011 Canadian consensus reported more than 200 distinct ethnic origins, including *Canadian*. In lines with the data of the consensus, approximately 21 percent of Canadians were born outside of the country, while 93.5 percent of the total could converse both in their mother tongue and in the official language.

The Multiculturalism Policy in Canada

As we already noted, in 1971, Canada officially voiced its commitment to the concept of multiculturalism. On that note, a formal policy has been created in order to safeguard and promote diversity, acknowledge the rights of Aboriginal peoples, and encourage the use of Canada's two official languages. This contributed to the establishment of the Ministry of Multiculturalism in 1973, and the Canadian Consultative Council on Multiculturalism.

[69]

The concept was, once again, included in the Charter of Rights and Freedoms of 1982. That highlighted that the Charter ought to be conveyed in a manner that was relevant to the enhancement and preservation of the multicultural heritage of the Canadians.

The *Canadian Multiculturalism Act* (21 July 1988) outlined the government's determination to encourage the equitable and full participation of communities and individuals of all origins in shaping the uniqueness of the Canadian culture.

The multiculturalism policies didn't address the needs of all immigrants. To some extent, they met the specifications of the long-established ethnic groups of European background. Nevertheless, the introduction of the concept and the fact that it has been recognized as the multicultural movement highlighted the *necessity* of assessing Canada's diversity.

How did the public react to these policies? At first, these policies have been conveyed with suspicion and hostility. For instance, a range of French Canadians thought of the policies as being prejudicial to the French Canadian status. Notwithstanding, there were suspicion and hostility regarding multiculturalism, due to the ambiguities present in the policy statements.

Still, it's worth noting that Canada was actually the first country that adopted multiculturalism in the form of official policy. The *immigrants* that reached Canada beginning from Jacques Cartier until today relish harmony, peace, fairness, and freedom – this is one of the main elements that characterize the Canadian culture.

Misconceptions about Canadian Culture

1. Everyone in Canada Speaks French

It's 100 percent accurate that the French have played a crucial role in the shaping of the Canadian culture. Notwithstanding, this doesn't necessarily imply that all Canadians speak French, although this is a popular misconception.

Even though it's true that most provinces incorporate French-speaking communities, only 22 percent of the Canadians consider French as their first language. What is more, the majority of French speakers live in Quebec, where 95 percent of the total amount of population talks French, as a first or second language. Apart from this area, the French language is rarer.

2. Canada Has No Culture

This is, possibly, the most commonly met misinterpretation regarding Canadian culture. As we already discussed before, multiculturalism is one of the primary elements that characterize Canada. In this respect, Canada has a shared culture as well as various distinct regional cultures that make it unique in the entire world. By no means can one argue that Canada has no culture just because it encompasses a conglomeration of distinct elements that construct it.

That being said, we could say that Canadian culture is featured by a strong belief in multinational complexity. The cultural diversity, combined with the vastness of the geographical landscape and other elements make it challenging for one to define Canada. Nevertheless, that doesn't translate into the fact that this beautiful, unique country lacks cultural identity.

Interesting Facts about Canadian Culture

- Canadians celebrate Thanksgiving earlier than their American neighbors. More precisely, this holiday takes place the second Monday in October. What is more, the first time the Canadians celebrated Thanksgiving was in Newfoundland, in 1578, in comparison to the Americans who celebrated it in 1621. Interestingly enough, the date of this holiday has been changed several times until the Parliament finalized the day and the month in 1957.

- *A Mari Usque Ad Mare* accounts for a significant Canadian motto. It stands for *From Sea to Sea.*
- The literacy rate in Canada is over 99 percent.

If The Choice Were Yours

- What is your opinion regarding the Canadian Multiculturalism Act? Would you have adopted the same act if it were your choice? What factors would have helped you in making the right decision?

Chapter 7 - Ottawa and Other Things to See in Canada

Being the second largest country in the world, Canada has its share of astounding natural landscapes and special places for travelers to discover. This country is the homeland to culturally vibrant cities, which are surrounded by natural wonders. It could be said that no other place on earth provides the same diversity of adventures and experiences as Canada.

Characterized by a particular vibe of positivity, Canada includes a conglomeration of dynamic cities that have earned their reputation for promoting impeccable politeness and inclusiveness. So, if you do visit this stunning country, make sure you don't miss visiting the following places.

Ottawa

Ottawa is described as dynamic, colorful, lively, and friendly. Enclosed in natural splendor and characterized by a typical relaxed urban vibe, Ottawa is a genuinely unique traveling destination that will make you fall in love with it.

Canada's capital incorporates a wide range of important museums and monuments that speak of this country's history. Simply put, Ottawa gives visitors the chance to enjoy what is best about Canada in one place. The beautiful countryside in the proximity of Canada represents the perfect getaway if you want to see a distinct side of this country.

Canada's enormous Gothic Parliament buildings majestically embellish the downtown core, an inspiring assortment of districts around the Rideau Canal.

You should also go to the Winterlude Festival, which displays a bunch of magnificent ice sculptures.

So, whether it's winter, spring, summer or fall, Ottawa is a beautiful destination that will make you get acquainted with Canada's rich past.

Niagara Falls

It is implied that Niagara Falls is one of this country's most renowned natural wonders, attracting millions of travelers from all over the world. In truth, Niagara Falls has represented a major attraction for daredevils and tourists for over a century.

As a matter of fact, between the 19th and 20th centuries, several attempts of plunging over the falls have been noted.

Over the years, the town of Niagara Falls has embraced a typical carnival vibe. This lively, colorful atmosphere remains until today.

It is situated at approximately one hour's drive from Toronto, in the proximity of the American border. You'll be able to see the falls from a surprisingly close distance, more exactly from the edge.

Banff National Park and The Rocky Mountains

Banff National Park is located in the heart of the majestic Rocky Mountains, more exactly, in the province of Alberta. It displays Canada's most breathtaking scenery and natural landscapes. Snow-capped mountain tops, turquoise green lakes, and glaciers are some of the highlights that feature this spectacular park. Nevertheless, the crown of this park is Lake Louise. When you see the green waters mirroring the beautiful surrounding mountains, it'll feel like out-of-this-world.

Make sure you schedule a drive from Lake Louise to Jasper, as it will account for another unforgettable experience, when in Canada. Banff is also a popular area for winter sports, being the home to two of Canada's most popular ski destinations, namely Sunshine Village and Lake Louise Ski Resort.

Old Quebec

Old Quebec is renowned as a UNESCO World Heritage Site, and it's not too difficult to comprehend why. It encompasses the Upper and Lower Town of Quebec, and it features the city's most important historical buildings.

Along the St. Lawrence River, there is the Lower Town, which was the original home and establishment of the one and only Château Frontenac as well as other equally valuable treasures. The Upper Town is located on high cliffs, where you can find the Plains of Abraham, the Citadel, the Parque Historique de L'Artillerie and Place d'Armes.

Truth be told, this represents one of Canada's most significant historical areas. As a result, it is well developed for tourism. Apart from the historical sites, travelers can also choose from a wide range of museums, quaint shops, and restaurants.

Old Montreal

Montreal is an unexpected yet charming combination of old and new. The old section of Montreal, however, represents a major draw since it is soaked with so much history. The beautiful historic buildings gladly receive visitors with fine dining and multiple shopping options. Additionally, you could get a horse-drawn carriage to take you through the city.

The new part of Montreal is a modern, lively city, being in

utter contrast with old Montreal that attracts numerous tourists that want to decipher its authentic charm and distinct old-town atmosphere. Some of the must-see places you should include on your itinerary are the landmark Marché Bonsecours, the majestic Notre-Dame Basilica, the 1870s City Hall, the colorful Place Jacques-Cartier, and the memorable Rue Bonsecours.

Gros Morne National Park

In contrast with the greater majority of National Parks based in Canada, Gros Morne National Park is situated in a remote location. Nevertheless, it is still worth the effort as it enables you to uncover the astounding landscape comprising of imposing mountains and fjords.

It is acknowledged as a UNESCO World Heritage Site encompassing waterfalls, steep cliff walls, and incredible rock formations developed by the glacier waters. The landscapes you are bound to appreciate here are unique and majestic: some of the best Canada has to offer.

Many visitors choose to take a boat tour in order to uncover the hidden beauties of the scenery. Nevertheless, if you're an adventure enthusiast, you could also embark on one of the many hiking trails or, even better, give kayaking a shot. Even though during the winter the number of travelers slightly decreases, it is still open for ski touring, as there are numerous backcountry ski huts.

Conclusion

Canada is a country that was built as a result of the numerous qualities of its peoples, its stunning natural landscapes and riches and geographical position. It is crystal clear that Canada has been largely influenced by the stronger nations located in its proximity.

As a result, we cannot discuss a uniquely Canadian culture; on the opposite, this country has incorporated multiculturalism as a primary value. Immigration had an important impact on Canada, as it has enriched it, although some might say that this has actually made Canada renounce its original identity. But, to my mind, that is one of the primary elements that make it unique.

It has welcomed immigrants irrespective of cultural and ethnic background, in this way promoting equality, tolerance, and acceptance – the grounds for a modern society. Canada's position as the second largest country in the world highlights that it could upgrade its position in the world, and it *could* play a more important role.

In closing this book, I would like to note that multicultural and multinational Canada could provide quintessential guidance. Although it could be conveyed more as a civilization than a nation-state, we could learn a lot from it. We could understand how diverse people with different backgrounds can coexist in peace, tolerance, and freedom. This is something to look up to especially in the 21st century.

Made in the USA
San Bernardino, CA
07 February 2018